N for what?

My Kid Words Series (Book N)

Learn 30 Words Starting with Letter N and Learn Little Information about those Words.

N for Nuts

A nut is a hard-shelled fruit of some plants. They are an important part of human and animal diets. Nuts are natural power-packs of nutrients like vitamins, minerals, antioxidants, healthy fats, protein and fiber which help children grow, develop and learn.

N for Nopales

They are eaten as a vegetable in Mexico after the spines have been removed. Nopales have a moist crunchy texture with a slightly slimy texture similar to okra. In terms of flavor, they are tart, with a slightly citrusy taste.

N for Nuggets

A nuggets or chicken nugget is a food product consisting of a small piece of deboned chicken meat that is breaded or battered, then deep-fried or baked. Invented in the 1950s, chicken nuggets have become a very popular fast food restaurant item, as well as widely sold frozen for home use.

N for Noodles

Noodles are a staple food in many cultures. They are made from unleavened dough which is stretched, extruded, or rolled flat and cut into one of a variety of shapes.

N for Necklaces

A necklace is an article of jewellery that is worn around the neck. Necklaces may have been one of the earliest types of adornment worn by humans.

N for Nightie

A nightgown, nightie or nightdress is a loosely hanging item of nightwear and is commonly worn by women and girls. A nightgown is made from cotton, silk, satin, or nylon

N for Night

Nighttime is when the sun is on the other side of the Earth from you, and its light and heat don't get to you. We get day and night because the Earth spins (or rotates) on an imaginary line called its axis and different parts of the planet are facing towards the Sun or away from it.

N for Nylon

Nylon is an artificial fiber. It is one of the most commonly used polyamides and was first produced on February 28, 1935. Nylon makes a silky material which was first used in toothbrushes. It is strong, hard and water resistant. It is used to make clothes, ropes and many more.

N for Nails

The use of nails dates back to ancient times, and they are believed to have originated in Mesopotamia as early as 3500 BCE. The first nails were most likely made out of copper of bronze, and nails would later be made out of iron.

N for Needle

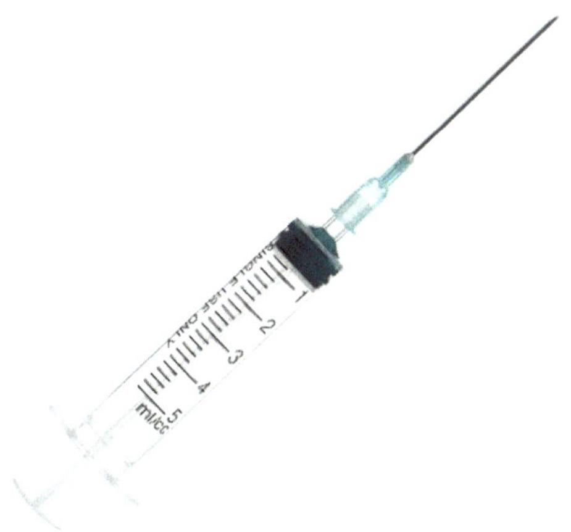

A needle is a thin hollow metal rod with a sharp point, which is part of a medical instrument called a syringe. It is used to put a drug into someone's body, or to take blood out.

N for Nail cutter

A nail clipper (also called nail clippers, a nail trimmer, a nail cutter or nipper type) is a hand tool used to trim fingernails, toenails and hangnails.

N for Notebook

A notebook (also known as a notepad, writing pad, drawing pad, or legal pad) is a book or stack of paper pages that are often ruled and used for purposes such as note-taking, journaling or other writing, drawing, or scrapbooking.

N for Ninja

Ninjas were Japanese fighters who lived in Japan about 700 years ago. These warriors were originally called shinobi-no-mono. Also, Ninjas were not just fighters, they were fighters who were also spies!! Ninjas received special training from very young age.

N for Nintendo

The Nintendo is a hybrid video game console developed by Nintendo and released worldwide in most regions on March 3, 2017. The console itself is a tablet that can either be docked for use as a home console or used as a portable device, making it a hybrid console.

N for Nasal spray

Nasal sprays are liquid medicines you spray into your nose. They are used to help relieve congestion (stuffiness) in your nose. Congestion is often a symptom of a cold or allergies.

N for Napkin

A napkin is a piece of cloth used for wiping your mouth while you're eating or drinking. Your grandmother might insist that everyone put their napkins in their laps before dinner is served.

N for Neon lamp

A neon lamp is a light bulb that can make many colors when Noble gasses are inside of the bulb. For example, helium would give a light yellow color and neon would make a red or orange color when an electric current is run in the tube. It is normally used to make letters for signs.

N for Newspaper

A newspaper is a publication printed on paper and issued regularly, usually once a day or once a week. It gives information and opinions written by journalists about current events and news. Scholars commonly credit the ancient Romans with publishing the first newspaper, Acta Diurna, or daily doings, in 59 BCE.

N for Numbers

A number. is a basic unit of mathematics. Numbers are used for counting, measuring, and comparing amounts. A number system is a set of symbols, or numerals, that are used to represent numbers. The most common number system uses 10 symbols called digits—0, 1, 2, 3, 4, 5, 6, 7, 8, and 9—and combinations of these digits.

N for Nine

In mathematics, the number 9 represents a quantity or value of 9. Example; here are 9 balloons, 9 ducklings, and 9 bunches of cherries.

N for Nurse

Nurses give medicine, change bandages, help patients move around, and provide other treatment. They give advice on how to get well and how to stay healthy. They comfort frightened patients and worried family members. Many nurses specialize in a certain area. Some nurses assist doctors during surgery.

N for Nose

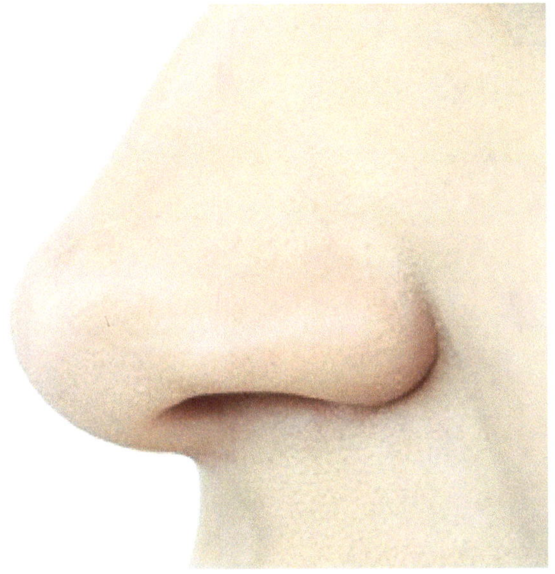

Your nose is part of your respiratory system. It allows air to enter your body, then filters debris and warms and moistens the air. Your nose gives you a sense of smell and helps shape your appearance.

N for Neck

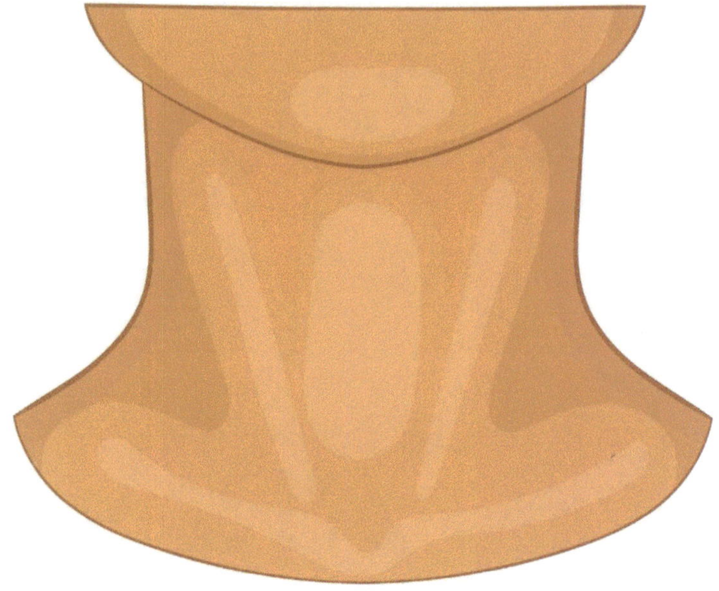

The neck is the part of the body on many vertebrates that connects the head with the torso. The neck supports the weight of the head and protects the nerves that carry sensory and motor information from the brain down to the rest of the body.

N for Nape

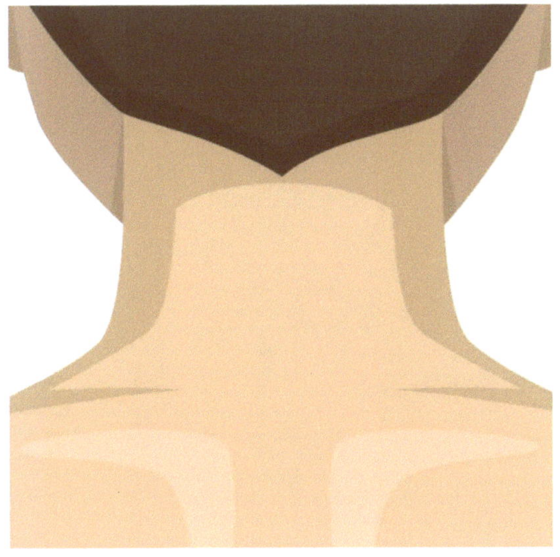

The nape is the back of the neck. In many mammals, the nape is the site of the scruff, a loose, non-sensitive area of skin by which the mother can carry her young, holding the scruff between her teeth.

N for Nail plate

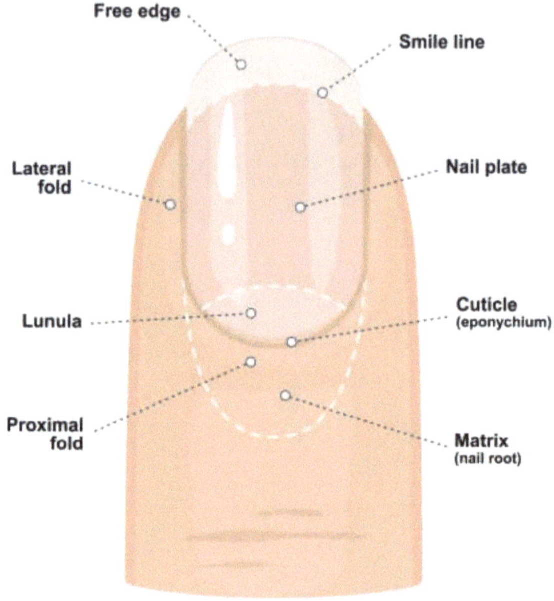

A nail or nail plate is a hard part of the body at the tip of the fingers and toes, of which most people have ten. Toenails and fingernails are similar, except that toenails grow four times slower. Only certain mammals have nails: mostly, they are found in primates.

N for Nervous

If someone is nervous, they are frightened or worried about something that is happening or might happen and show this in their behavior.

N for Nature

Nature is all the animals, plants, and other things in the world that are not made by people, and all the events and processes that are not caused by people.

N for Nest

A nest is a structure in which an animal lives or keeps its young. Birds are well known for building nests for their eggs. Some fish, amphibians, reptiles, mammals, and insects also build nests.

N for Number plate

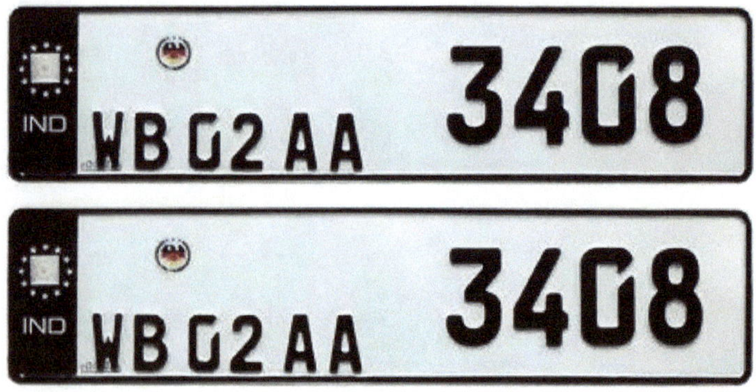

A number plate, also known as a, license plate, or license plate, vehicle registration plate is a metal or plastic plate attached to a motor vehicle or trailer for official identification purposes. All countries require registration plates for road vehicles such as cars, trucks, and motorcycles.

N for Neptune

It's the last of the planets in our solar system. It's more than 30 times as far from the sun as Earth is. Neptune is very similar to Uranus. It's made of a thick fog of water, ammonia, and methane over an Earth-sized solid center. Its atmosphere is made of hydrogen, helium, and methane. The average distance from Neptune to Earth is 2.703 billion miles.

A for what?
My Kid Words Series
(Book A)
B for what?
My Kid Words Series
(Book B)
C for what?
My Kid Words Series
(Book C)
D for what?
My Kid Words Series
(Book D)
E for what?
My Kid Words Series
(Book E)
F for what?
My Kid Words Series
(Book F)
G for what?
My Kid Words Series
(Book G)
H for what?
My Kid Words Series
(Book H)
I for what?
My Kid Words Series
(Book I)
Many More Books
A to Z (26 books)